WISDOM
of
ALPACAS

MOSELEY ROAD INC.
International Rights and Packaging
22 Knollwood Avenue
Elmsford, NY 10523
www.moseleyroad.com

President: Sean Moore
Editor: Finn Moore
Art director and photo research: Grace Moore
Printed in China

ISBN 978-1-62669-150-6

WISDOM
of
ALPACAS

Compiled by
Grace Moore

Moseley Road, Inc.
Elmsford, New York

"I am no bird;
and no net
ensnares me:

"Happiness is something that comes into our lives through doors we don't even remember leaving open."

- ROSE LANE

"No act of kindness, no matter how small, is ever wasted."

- AESOP

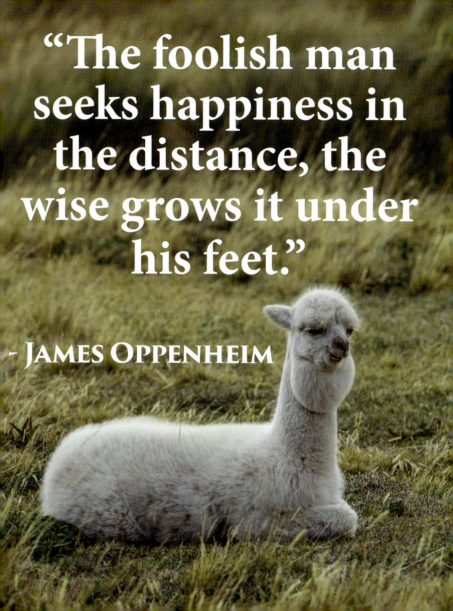

"The foolish man seeks happiness in the distance, the wise grows it under his feet."

- JAMES OPPENHEIM

"I'd far rather be happy than right any day."

- DOUGLAS ADAMS

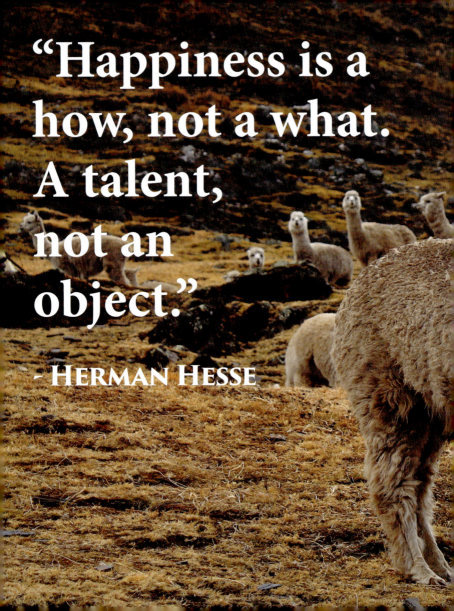

"Since you get more joy out of giving joy to others, you should put a good deal of thought into the happiness that you are able to give."

- ELEANOR ROOSEVELT

"A table, a chair, a bowl of fruit and a violin; what else does a man need to be happy?"

- ALBERT EINSTEIN

"It's been my experience that you can nearly always enjoy things if you make up your mind firmly that you will."

- L. M. MONTGOMERY

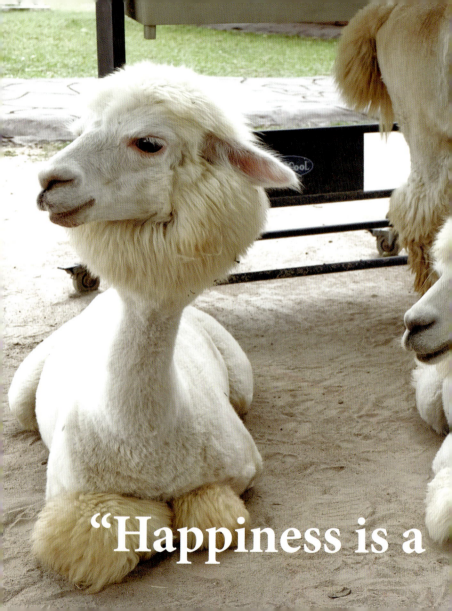

"Happiness is a

state of activity."
- ROSE LANE

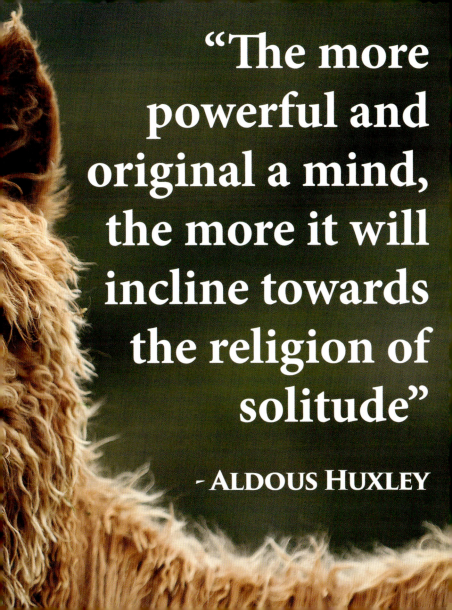

"The more powerful and original a mind, the more it will incline towards the religion of solitude"

- ALDOUS HUXLEY

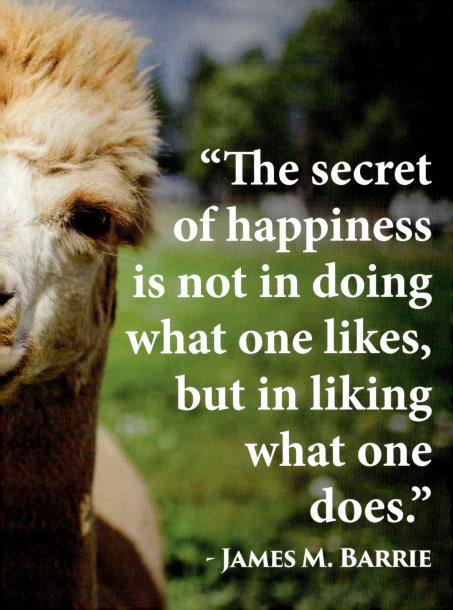

"The secret of happiness is not in doing what one likes, but in liking what one does."

- JAMES M. BARRIE

"The greatest thing in the world is to know how to belong to oneself."

- MICHEL DE MONTAIGNE

"Happiness is not the mere possession of money; it lies in the joy of achievement, in the thrill of creative effort."

- FRANKLIN D. ROOSEVELT

"Freedom lies in being bold."

- ROBERT FROST

"The unhappiest people in this world, are those who care the most about what other people think."

- C. JOYBELLE C.

"Freeing yourself was one thing, claiming ownership of that freed self was another."

- TONI MORRISON

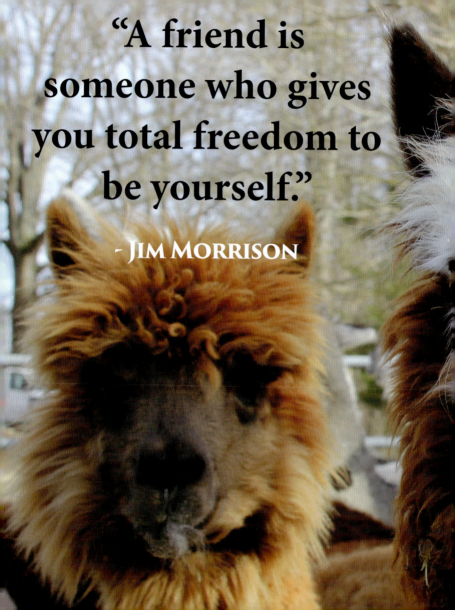

"A friend is someone who gives you total freedom to be yourself."

- JIM MORRISON

"I am free, no matter what rules surround me. If I find them tolerable, I tolerate them; if I find them too obnoxious, I break them. I am free because I now that I alone am morally responsible for everything I do."

- ROBERT A. HEINLEIN

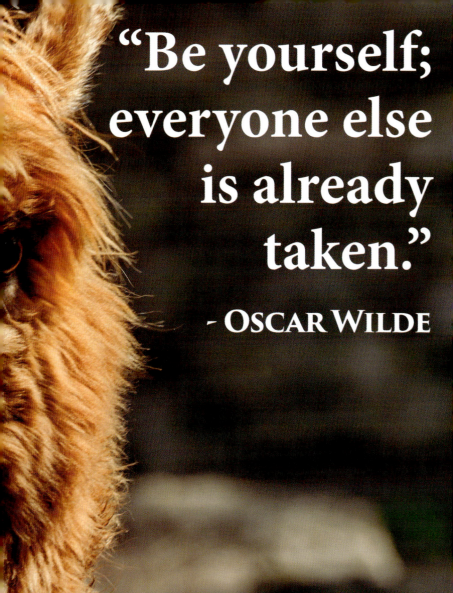

"No one loses anyone, because no one owns anyone. That is the true experience of freedom: having the most important thing in the world without owning it."

- PAULO COELHO

"The first duty of a man is to think for himself."

- JOSÉ MARTÍ

"To go wrong in one's own way is better than to go right in someone else's."

- FYODOR DOSTOYEVSKY

"I, not events, have the power to make me happy or unhappy today. I can choose which it shall be.

Yesterday is dead, tomorrow hasn't arrived yet. I have just one day, today, and I'm going to be happy in it."

- GROUCHO MARX

"Inside us there is something that has no name, that something is what we are."

- JOSÉ SARAMAGO

"**When you are content to be simply yourself and don't compare or compete, everyone will respect you.**"

- LAO TZU

"If I ever go looking for my heart's desire again, I won't look any further than by own backyard. Because if it isn't there, I never really lost it to begin with."

- L. FRANK BAUM

"The easiest thing in the world is to be you. The most difficult thing to be is what other people want you to be. Don't let them put you in that position."

- LEO BUSCAGLIA

"He who is satisfied with little, is satisfied with nothing."

- EPICURUS

"To be yourself in a world that is constantly trying to make you something else is the greatest accomplishment.

- RALPH WALDO EMERSON

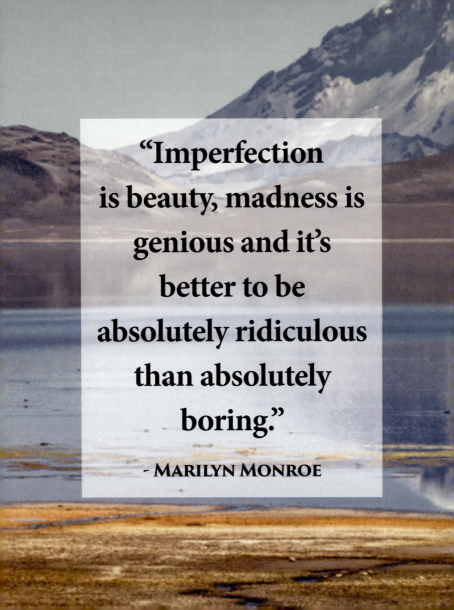

"Remember to always be yourself.

Unless you suck."

- JOSS WHEDON

"Follow your heart, listen to your inner voice, stop caring about what others think.

- ROY T. BENNETT

"Always be the first rate version of yourself and not the second rate version of someone else.

- JUDY GARLAND

"I'm not in this world to live up to your expectations and you're not in this world to live up to mine."

- BRUCE LEE

"Follow your inner moonlight; don't hide the madness."

- ALLEN GINSBERG

"The surest way to corrupt a youth is to instruct him to hold in higher esteem those who think alike than those who think differently."

- FRIEDRICH NIETZSCHE

"In order to be irreplaceable, one must always be different."

- COCO CHANEL

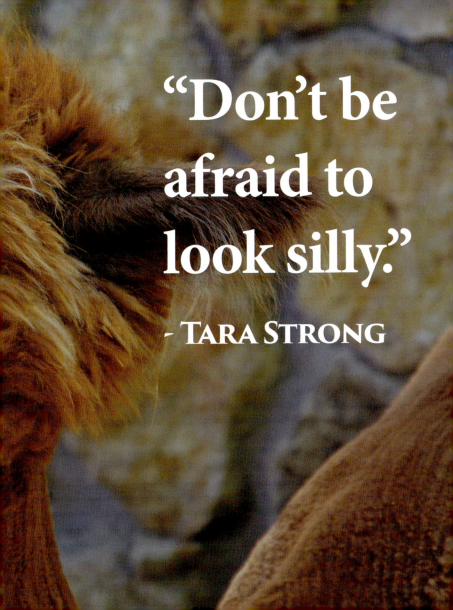

"Don't be afraid to look silly."

- TARA STRONG

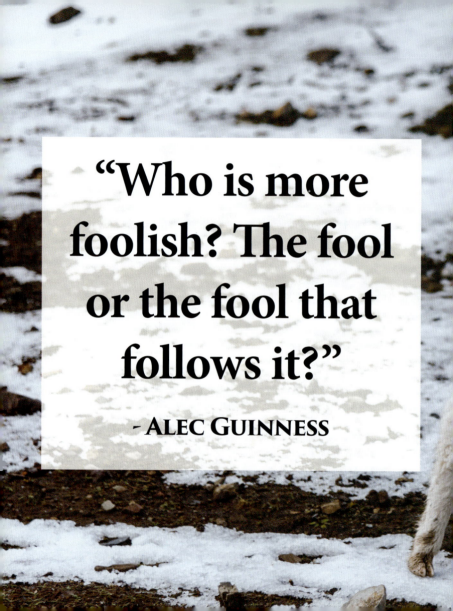

"Who is more foolish? The fool or the fool that follows it?"

- ALEC GUINNESS

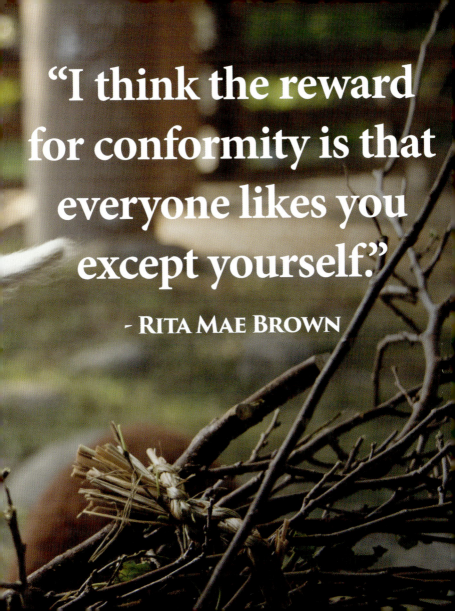

"I think the reward for conformity is that everyone likes you except yourself."

- RITA MAE BROWN

"Never be bullied into silence. Never allow yourself to be made a victim. Accept on one's definition of your life, but define yourself."

- HARVEY FIERSTEIN

"The individual has always had to struggle to keep from being overwhelmed by the tribe. If you try it, you will be lonely often, and sometimes frightened. But no price is too high to pay for the privilege of owning yourself."

- FRIEDRICH NIETZSCHE

"Whenever a man does a thoroughly stupid thing,

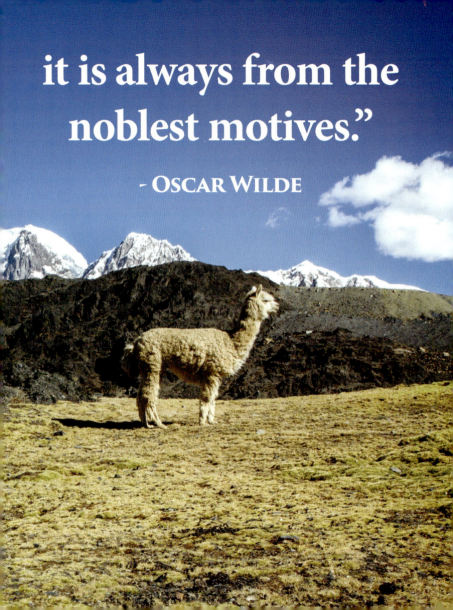

"Until you're ready to look foolish, you'll never have the possibility of being great."

- CHER

"You may not control all the events that happen to you, but you can decide not to be reduced by them."

- MAYA ANGELOU

"You cannot change what you are, only what you do."

‐ PHILIP PULLMAN

"Be yourself,
don't take
anything
from anyone,
and never let
them take you
alive."

- GERARD WAY

"I didn't like the idea of being foolish, but I learned pretty soon that it was essential to fail and be foolish."

- DANIEL DAY-LEWIS

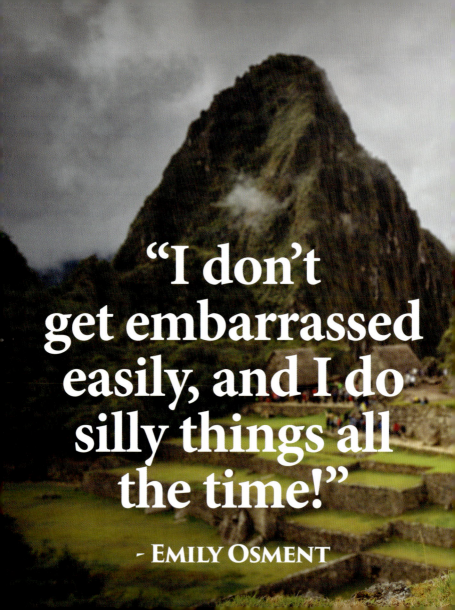

"I don't get embarrassed easily, and I do silly things all the time!"

— EMILY OSMENT

"People who do not wish to appear foolish; to avoid the appearance of foolishness, they are willing to remain actually fools."

- ALICE WALKER

"I, myself, am made entirely of flaws, stitched together with good intentions."

- AUGUSTEN BURROUGHS

"You will do foolish things, but do them with enthusiasm."

- COLETTE

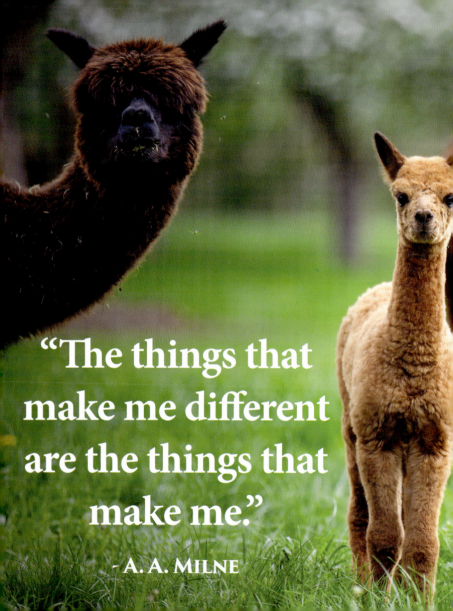

"The things that make me different are the things that make me."

- A. A. MILNE

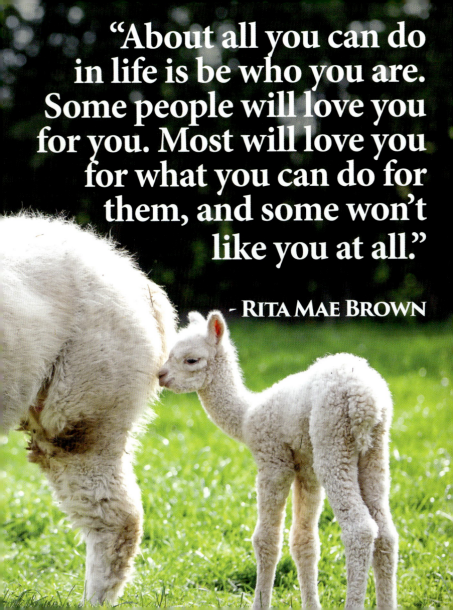

"About all you can do in life is be who you are. Some people will love you for you. Most will love you for what you can do for them, and some won't like you at all."

- RITA MAE BROWN

PICTURE CREDITS